101 Fantasy and Sci-Fi Writing Prompts

Crystal Raen

ISBN-10: 1533135320
ISBN-13: 978-1533135322

DEDICATION

For my husband and daughter. The former for always being tolerant of my whims, the latter, just for being. I love you both dearly.

CONTENTS

INTRODUCTION

First, I want to say thank you for picking up this awesome book full of writing prompts. If you've been following my work, then you know that I can definitely relate to anyone who suffers from writing block. In an attempt to cure my own writers block I gave myself the task of creating 101 writing prompts for myself to use. Luckily for you, I thought it would be a shame not to share them with other writers. I decided to just have fun and I've created prompts that are funny, cliché, and serious (not all at once mind you).

For those of you who do not follow my work and thought that this workbook was what you needed in your life anyway, I just want to say Hello! I am Crystal Raen. I have self-published one novel, *Child of Galina*, one book of poetry, *More than Fear: A Poetry Collection*, and I've had a poem published in *Book of the Tribes: A Tribute to Clive Barker* by various artists and authors. In the "real world" I have worked on various company blogs creating content for their readers. I can be found on Facebook and at www.crystalraen.com.

I hope that these writing prompts come in handy for you. I want to stress that the best strategy to using this workbook is to just have fun with it. Oftentimes the key to breaking through writer's block is to just force your hand to write, even if the words are not necessarily ones you plan on using in your next big project.

And, one more thing, these prompts are for you. So, if a character's name, gender, age, etc. doesn't work for you in the initial writing prompt, grab some whiteout and change it. If the prompt gives you a completely different idea that you are excited to work on instead of that particular prompt, cross it out and go with your own thing.

Seriously, you can write all over this workbook, or keep it pristine. Use it for short stories, the beginnings of stories, to do a timeline/layout/story map, whatever, just let it help you get those creative juices flowing. Decide you'd rather doodle? It is your book, feel free.

And don't hesitate to share what you've created from these writing prompts with others. Sometimes a second opinion can help you to see paths you wouldn't have taken before.

I hope this book is what you need to get you going.

PEN (or pencil, the choice really is yours anyway) IN HAND, TURN THE PAGE, AND LET'S BEGIN

1. I never believed witches existed. Then I met Alex…

2. The city was sparkling in the night. It seemed to be a beautiful, living thing that no one thought twice about. No one but me anyway…

3. "Careful! Don't make the plants bleed."…

4. The sheep stood their ground while chanting "Down with the wolf! Down with the Wolf!"...

5. No normal robber could have pulled this heist off. No normal robber could survive…

6. The building was dark and smelled of electricity…

7. The steel of his sword blazed in the sun as he brought it
down with a thunk…

_____

_____

_____

_____

_____

_____

_____

_____

_____

_____

_____

_____

_____

_____

_____

_____

_____

_____

_____

_____

8. She could have passed for normal, if not for her pointed ears…

9. The water shimmered purple and gold. She hauled the net into her boat. It was heavy and she gasped…

10. It had taken them 40 years to get here, but you wouldn't know that by looking at them…

11. From the corner of his eye he caught movement inside
    the painting…

12. "The patients here do not realize that they are patients. They believe they are living a normal life out in the world. While you are employed here, you must maintain that illusion."…

13. The noises inside the wall seemed to get louder as the crack in the plaster began to grow…

14. The land was a barren place, except for a weeping willow tree in the distance…

15. They came upon us from the sky. That is when we first learned of violence. Before that night, the term did not even exist here…

16. "The dragon was hunting for you. He was through here earlier today."…

17. There was a loud knock at the door. When Julia went to answer, no one was there, but a large box was on the stoop…

18. The meeting seemed to be lasting for hours. The hunger inside of her was growing, she needed to leave before…

19. He pulled into the empty parking lot. "Where is everyone" he wondered…

20. There is only one magical creature left in the world. That magical creature is you…

21. There is only one NON-magical creature left in the world. That creature is you…

22. Extreme displays of emotion are punishable by death. You have just witnessed a murder…

23. Life vacations are currently all the rage. You work at a company that specializes in permanent life vacations. You help clients create new identities and lives for their "vacation". Then you use magic to erase them from the memories of those who know them in their current life. Your next customer just walked through the door. It is the president…

24. A hypnotist discovers that he can cause people to have super powers as a side effect of their sessions with him…

25. Tell a UFO abduction tale from the perspective of the family pet.

26. Massive companies are capturing witches and forcing them to work in their factories.

27. The most powerful magician the world has ever seen has just had his heart broken by a mere human.

28. You discover that your body is literally a theme park with thousands of tiny creatures (invisible to the human eye) visiting each day.

29. Write a fantasy/sci-fi story using every stereotype you can think of.

30. You accidentally discover that you are a shape shifter while you are giving a presentation at a magical suppression seminar.

31. You can create magical creatures using corpse parts from different animals…

32. Your devoutly religious protagonist receives a message from their god through a lady bug. The lady bug gives them a task to carry out…

33. The ocean was vast and beautiful, but beware the
creatures that crawl out at night…

34. The letter was unexpected, she never received mail. Her aunt ripped it away from her before she could read it. "Anything for you belongs in the garbage." Her aunt tore the letter up and deposited into the trash can.

35. Amongst the thousands who wanted their names to be called, it is your name that sounds out over the intercom…

36. "They lied you know."
   "What?" Dylan was startled from his thoughts.
   "We're not crazy, what happened was real."
   "Who are you?" Dylan asked.

37. Prison changed Maggie, all she wanted upon her release was a cold beer. But on her way to the bar a man approached her…

38. Rumor is, at the bottom of the pond there's a mirror. A mirror that leads to another world. So far, no one who has tried to visit has ever resurfaced…

39. Ronald has accidentally freed an evil overlord…

40. Robot companions have replaced human relationships…

41. His tattoos began to come to life, and the things they were saying…

42. The zombie apocalypse happened years ago. There are a few human survivors after all this time. You are among them, living in a crude encampment…

43. The pain was indescribable, but brief. And the results, well they were so worth it…

44. Lately, you've noticed when you day dream about certain things, the world around you seems to be effected by your thoughts. Your day dreams don't really come true in the way you imagine though…

45. An experiment went wrong in a major way. To cover up, the lab let all the experiments loose in the "wilds" of Houston, Texas.

46. The door was tiny, only 10 inches tall, and hidden at the back of the hall closet. Every night at 1:00 a.m. light could be seen shining around the door's edges.

47. Describe a world where humans are the pets of another species.

48. Identities are being stolen, but not in the way that one would normally expect…

49. Society has banned time. There are no clocks and no dates, so no marked holidays or celebrations ever come to pass. There is a secret sect who are continuing to keep time so that Earth's history can be kept accurately. They have invited you to become a member…

50. It is discovered that those who held beliefs that photos capture pieces of the soul were correct. Now, with enough photographs of a person who has passed away, you can bring them back from the dead…

51. A new religious sect has emerged, they have discovered how to utilize all of the brain's capacity. This has given them super powers. How will they use these powers?

52. People are evolving, a new sense is emerging. This sense...

53. Events in history are changing, Joey is the only person who realizes this. Everyone else's memories are being replaced by this new past…

54. It is discovered that plants communicate with one another on a highly intellectual level, we can now understand their communications…

55. The kids tried to convince themselves that what they had done was for a good cause. But deep down, they knew that was a lie…

56. The toadstools were as big as houses and I couldn't help…

57. Things were always different at night for Lara. Because of this she was never able to attend sleepovers. But tonight she was having a friend over for the first time.

58. The world hasn't changed much. Not in the grand scheme of things…

59. The bones were propped up on the mantle like trophies…

60. Sue stood at her stoop confused. Her door was still there, but the house? Gone without a trace…

61. Kissing frogs is for the birds, but if you needed an eye of newt, she is the girl for you…

62. The bird dropped the red stone on the window sill. He tapped his beak on the pane before flying away…

63. The horizon was aflame. The glass buildings had been constructed for just this event. Now they would see if their engineers were worth their salary…

64. You are working for the historical society scanning documents. You come across one set of folders that feel warm and are heavier than they should be…

65. She was getting ready to cross the street when she heard someone say "Do NOT cross here!"
She didn't see any people, just a scrappy cat sitting on the stoop of the museum…

66. The book seemed to be calling to her. She reached out and touched the leather binding. Instantly she was transported…

67. There were three prophesies that boldly contradicted one another. These prophesies divided the people in the world into four groups…

68. The village lay in the valley bathed in the light of the moon…

69. "Do you remember?"
    "Don't make me, the memories hurt."

70. The group entered the derelict institution. No one had been here for years. They were staying the night for a dare…

71. The words won't come, they are there inside my
    mouth, but I cannot speak. Everyone is waiting for…

72. You are living in an experimental community. Everyone knows the truth, except for you and the "others"…

73. After Susan's surgery, every time she sneezes she appears two months in the past. Susan just walked through a cloud of dust…

74. People are being kidnapped and used as pawns in a real-life virtual reality game. They are controlled by those who are "playing" the game…

75. An underground network of lizard people is the only thing keeping the center of the Earth from overheating and killing all life as we know it.

76. A community of Big Foot Creatures is discovered. They are drafted into the military to train servicemen in their camouflage techniques…

77. After her best friend's death Gail starts trying to track down a necromancer…

78. You are at a college for people with magical abilities. No one is turned away, good or evil. You've discovered your roommate tends toward the evil side in a major way…

79. An unexpected animal species suddenly has human intelligence and speech…

80. Suddenly humans can no longer see one another. Everyone thinks they are the last human on a very haunted Earth…

81. Something horrific came into town with the carnival...

82. She had just gone to bed when there was a rap at her door, she opened it to find a wizard who beckoned her to follow him…

83. It was a rather odd place, and she could swear that butterfly had bid her a good morning…

84. What if it were your dreams that were real?

85. It is the last civilization, on planet Xygonia the Humans are racing to find another habitable planet as they've drained this one of its resources. Rumors emerge that the original planet, Earth, has recovered.

86. A new door has appeared in your house. One you are quite sure was never there before…

87. The king of the Dragons has requested a meeting with the human leader. The emperor, being afraid, sends you in his place…

88. He lived his life believing he was the chosen, the only one who could save the world, only to discover he is normal, and the true chosen was never born…

89. You are walking through familiar woods when you notice the entrance of a cave that you'd never seen before. From within you hear a baby crying…

90. The city has been in lock down for a decade, but now, with food at its scarcest a team is being assembled to go out and bring back provisions, news, and new people…

91. The beast was feared by all. Silver and black it bellowed smoke and brought death and destruction wherever it went.

92. Tanya woke up from a dream about her childhood only to discover her favorite toys from that time are in her bedroom. The same toys that were lost in a fire 15 years ago…

93. Shipwrecked on a seemingly deserted island, you wander inwards towards the island's center. You come across an obviously ancient, deserted city, but the technology you discover is astounding...

94. You have traveled to the future and brought devastation with you in the form of pinkeye which is causing nearly instant blindness in those who come into contact with you…

95. Able to control the sun, the government becomes more like a big brother than ever believed possible…

96. A planet ruled by cats has been discovered by a space probe sent out to find life on another planet. How do they react to the rover that lands amongst them?

97. People are being categorized by their abilities and divided into groups. They are not allowed to interact with others from different sects in this new society…

98. A book of spells has mysteriously appeared on your bookshelf…

99. You realize your life is actually a book, if the current reader doesn't finish your story, you will cease to exist...

100. Your dream was strangely vivid, staying with you all day. Later, you are scrolling through images on your camera when you realize that some of those images could only be from your dream …

101. Pick up a book. Flip to a random page. Close your eyes and point to a random sentence. Use that sentence to start your next sci-fi or fantasy story.

NOTES:

ABOUT THE AUTHOR

Crystal Raen is the author of Child of Galina, More than Fear: A Poetry Collection, and has had a poem published in Book of the Tribes: A Tribute to Clive Barker. Crystal resides in the Appalachian Mountains of rural Southwest Virginia. She lives with her husband, daughter, and two furbabies of the feline variety.

You can learn more about Crystal at http://crystalraen.com

www.ingramcontent.com/pod-product-compliance
Lightning Source LLC
Chambersburg PA
CBHW081207280526
45787CB00006B/2354